Probability

Probability

BY CHARLES F. LINN   ILLUSTRATED BY WENDY WATSON

Thomas Y. Crowell Company   New York

YOUNG MATH BOOKS

Edited by Dr. Max Beberman, Director of the Committee on School Mathematics Projects, University of Illinois

BIGGER AND SMALLER by Robert Froman

CIRCLES by Mindel and Harry Sitomer

COMPUTERS by Jane Jonas Srivastava

THE ELLIPSE by Mannis Charosh

ESTIMATION by Charles F. Linn

FRACTIONS ARE PARTS OF THINGS
by J. Richard Dennis

GRAPH GAMES by Frédérique and Papy

LINES, SEGMENTS, POLYGONS
by Mindel and Harry Sitomer

LONG, SHORT, HIGH, LOW, THIN, WIDE
by James T. Fey

MATHEMATICAL GAMES FOR ONE OR TWO
by Mannis Charosh

ODDS AND EVENS by Thomas C. O'Brien

PROBABILITY by Charles F. Linn

RIGHT ANGLES: PAPER-FOLDING GEOMETRY
by Jo Phillips

RUBBER BANDS, BASEBALLS AND DOUGHNUTS:
A BOOK ABOUT TOPOLOGY by Robert Froman

STRAIGHT LINES, PARALLEL LINES,
PERPENDICULAR LINES by Mannis Charosh

WEIGHING & BALANCING by Jane Jonas Srivastava

WHAT IS SYMMETRY? by Mindel and Harry Sitomer

Edited by Dorothy Bloomfield, Mathematics Specialist, Bank Street College of Education

AREA by Jane Jonas Srivastava

GAME OF FUNCTIONS by Robert Froman

LESS THAN NOTHING IS REALLY SOMETHING
by Robert Froman

NUMBER IDEAS THROUGH PICTURES
by Mannis Charosh

SHADOW GEOMETRY by Daphne Harwood Trivett

SPIRALS by Mindel and Harry Sitomer

STATISTICS by Jane Jonas Srivastava

VENN DIAGRAMS by Robert Froman

L.C. Card 79-171006
ISBN 0-690-65601-7   0-690-65602-5 (LB)

3   4   5   6   7   8   9   10

Probability

YOUNG MATH BOOKS

Most likely you have heard the weatherman on television say something like this: "The chances of rain tomorrow are about 7 out of 10"; or, "The PROBABILITY of rain tomorrow is about 4 out of 10." Sometimes he says, "The probability of rain is about 1 in 10."

The weatherman gives these numbers to show that he uses mathematics in his work. He uses such words as "chances" and "probability" to show he cannot really be sure about tomorrow's weather. Weathermen and many other modern scientists use a kind of mathematics called PROBABILITY THEORY in their work. This is a kind of mathematics which gives scientists a way of predicting the weather, or what a large number of molecules will do, or what a large number of people will do. They use records of what has happened in the past to help them make their predictions.

Suppose the weatherman says: "The chances of rain tomorrow are about 7 out of 10." This means someone—probably a computer—has looked carefully over weather records of many years. The computer picked out those days on which weather conditions were very much like the weather conditions today. Then the computer looked at what kind of weather came on the following days.

There may have been 100 days with weather conditions very

much like today's. Maybe on 71 of those days, rain came the next day. So, the weatherman can say that in about 70 out of 100, or 7 out of 10, times, weather like today's was followed by rain.

Of course, the weatherman will check what kind of weather there really is tomorrow. He will add this information to the weather records. As the weather records grow, the weatherman can be more sure about his predictions. That is what probability theory is all about.

You can do some experiments that will help you understand how probability is used by scientists.

For the first experiment, you will need some thumbtacks. You can toss many tacks—say 20—a few times. Or, you can toss 5 or 10 tacks 40 or 20 times. But, toss tacks until you have about 200 throws altogether. Keep a record of how many tacks you toss and how many tacks land point up.

5

Susan and Meg decided to try the experiment themselves. "We'll get a lot of information faster by working together," they agreed. So they quickly built up the following table:

Tosses	Points up
卌 卌	卌 II

That is, of 200 thumbtacks tossed, 112 landed point up.

If you asked them what the chances are of a thumbtack landing point up on the next toss, they would say, "About 112 out of 200."

How many of your tacks landed point up? What is your prediction for the next tack you toss?

Now, try the same experiment again. Compare your two results.

I don't want to try it again.

It would be very surprising if your two answers are the same. You can expect them to be close, however. But how close?

Mathematicians try to answer such questions as "How close is 'close'?" with probability theory.

How close were your results to Susan and Meg's?

Or, maybe you used a different kind of thumbtack.

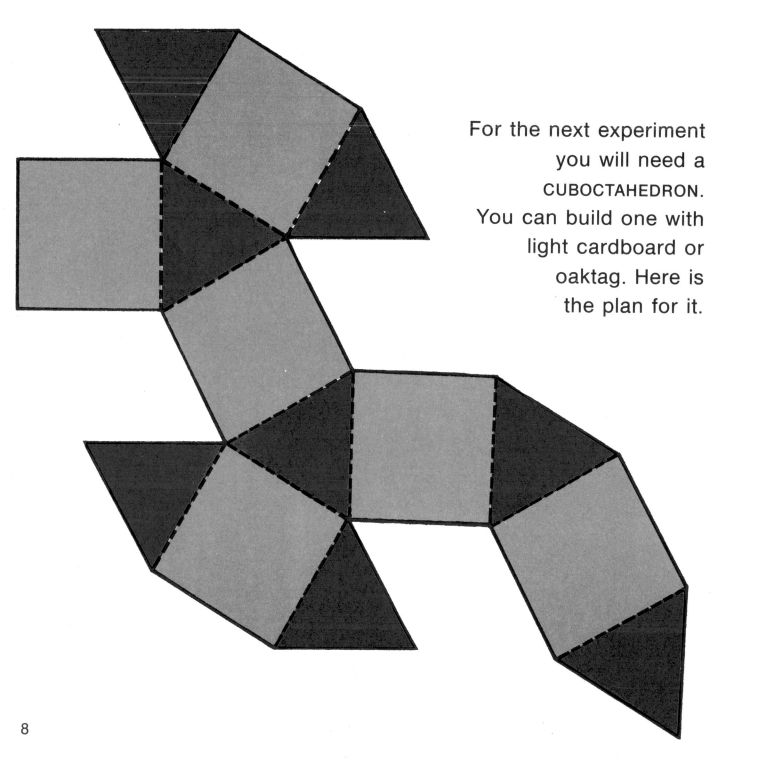

For the next experiment
you will need a
CUBOCTAHEDRON.
You can build one with
light cardboard or
oaktag. Here is
the plan for it.

Trace the plan onto thin paper and glue it onto the cardboard. Then, cut out the figure. Fold along the dotted lines. (It helps to score those dotted lines with scissors point and ruler before you fold.) Now, carefully tape the cuboctahedron together.

If you roll this cuboctahedron, what is the probability that it will land on one of the triangle faces?

One way to get an answer for this question is to roll the cuboctahedron many times. Keep a count of the number of times it lands on a triangle face.

Roll it 100 times. How many times did it land on a triangle?

20 times.

Now, roll it 100 times more. How many times did it land on a triangle?

Compare your two answers. How close are they?

Gordon and Bruce rolled a cuboctahedron back and forth across a table 1,000 times. It landed on triangles 211 times.

How do your answers compare with theirs?

From their experiment, they could say that the probability of their cuboctahedron landing on a triangle face is 211 out of 1,000.

20 out of 100 is about the same as 211 out of 1,000.

In the first two experiments, only two things could happen: the thumbtacks could land either point up or on the side; the cuboctahedron could land on a triangle or a square. In the next experiment, you will be tossing 10 coins at once. There are 11 things that can happen. Zero coins can land heads up; 1 coin can land heads up; 2 coins can land heads up; and so on, up to 10 heads. A mathematician would say there are 11 possible OUTCOMES. (You may prefer to count tails. The idea is the same.)

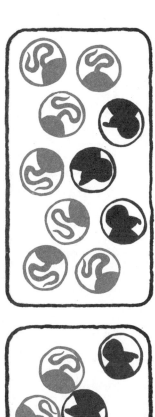

Before you begin tossing, you should make a chart
to keep score on. That chart may look like this:

Heads	Count
0	
1	
2	
3	
4	
5	
6	
7	
8	
9	
10	

Now, begin tossing the coins. Make a mark in your chart when you count the number of heads in each toss.

Heads	Count
0	
1	
2	I
3	
4	II
5	IIII I
6	I
7	
8	III
9	
10	

2 heads up.

Susan and Meg each tossed 10 coins 100 times. Then they put their answers together. Their final score looks like this:

Heads	Count	
0	/	1
1	//\	3
2	///// ///// /	11
3	///// ///// ///// ///// //	22
4	///// ///// ///// ///// ///// ///// ///// ///	38
5	///// ///// ///// ///// ///// ///// ///// ///// ///// ///	48
6	///// ///// ///// ///// ///// ///// ///// ///// //	42
7	///// ///// ///// ////	19
8	///// ///// //	12
9	////	4
10		0

Compare your record with theirs. In what ways are your charts and theirs alike? In what ways are they different?

Now, see if you can use the answers you gathered. If you were to toss 10 coins one more time, what number of heads is most likely to turn up?

5 HEADS

If you were to toss 10 coins another time, what is the probability that 7 heads would turn up?

19 OUT OF 200

What is the probability that between 3 and 7 heads would turn up when 10 coins are tossed?

___ OUT OF 200

You can do this same experiment with fewer or more than 10 coins. Have a try with, say, 6 coins. Maybe you can get friends to try this experiment with other numbers of coins. Each of you should keep a record like the one you kept for 10 coins. Compare your results. What predictions can you make, using this information you have collected?

6 Coins tossed 30 times

Heads	Count	
0		0
1	/	1
2	⊬⊬ ///	8
3	⊬⊬ ⊬⊬ //	12
4	⊬⊬ //	7
5	//	2
6		0

Even though I tossed fewer coins fewer times, my table looks like the other one. The middle line has the most marks.

No matter how many coins you toss, it is most likely half will turn up heads— MAYBE.

4 coins tossed 40 times

Heads	Count	
0		0
1	⊬⊬ |||	8
2	⊬⊬ ⊬⊬ ⊬⊬ ⊬⊬	20
3	⊬⊬ ||||	9
4					3

14 coins tossed 100 times

Heads	Count	
0		0
1		0
2		0
3				2
4	⊬⊬ ⊬⊬	10
5	⊬⊬ ||||	9
6	⊬⊬ ⊬⊬ ⊬⊬ ⊬⊬		21
7	⊬⊬ ⊬⊬ ||	12
8	⊬⊬ ⊬⊬ ⊬⊬ |||	18
9	⊬⊬ ⊬⊬ |||	13
10	⊬⊬ ||	7
11	⊬⊬	5
12					3
13		0
14		0

MAYBE is right! The experiment with 4 coins turned out about like the others, but what happened to the one with 14 coins?

Hmm — I guess you just don't always get perfect results.

Scientists often use GRAPHS when they show results from experiments. Graphs really change numbers into pictures.

If you have a piece of graph paper you can make a graph for the coin-tossing experiment. In Meg and Susan's graph they have a column of squares for each result, from zero heads to 10 heads.

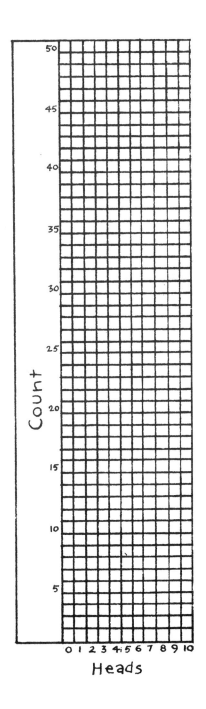

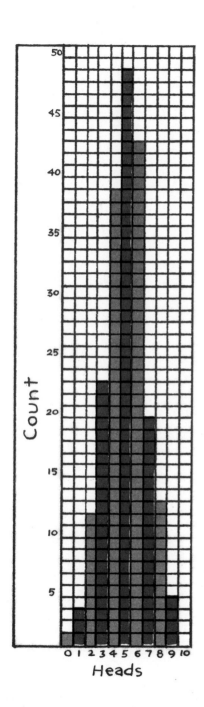

They colored in a square for each count.

In their "3 heads" column, they have 22 squares filled in. In their "6 heads" column, they have 42 squares filled in. And so on.

Their graph looks like this.

22

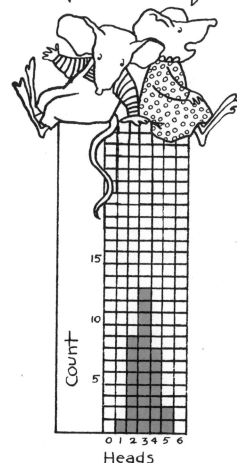

Here's a graph for the table of 6 coins tossed 30 times. It looks a lot like the others.

Graphs are good because we can compare results just by looking at pictures, instead of by reading lots of numbers.

Count

15

10

5

0 1 2 3 4 5 6

Heads

Compare your graph with theirs. If your friends are working on this experiment, you may want to compare your graph with theirs. Do you see why it is easier to compare graphs than to compare charts with numbers?

You may not have tossed the coins the same number of times that Meg and Susan did. But you still can compare the graphs. Do you see how the graphs can help you make predictions about another toss of 10 coins?

People take polls before an election to get an idea of who probably will win the election. They ask some people how they will vote. Then they use the results of this poll, or SAMPLING, to predict who will win the election.

Sampling is also used in industry. Sometimes the workers cannot test every single thing they make. So, checkers test only some of the things. This will give them an idea of about how many of the things are not good.

You can experiment with sampling. For the experiment you need something like this:

Many—oh, about 50 or 60—poker chips of two colors, say red and white; or marbles of two colors.

(I wanted to try this experiment one time when I did not have any poker chips or marbles. I dabbed a tiny bit of fast-drying paint—magic marker will do—on some pennies. Then I mixed these with unpainted pennies.)

Place the chips or marbles (or pennies) in a bag. (Don't count them—just dump them into a bag.) Shake them up. Now, draw out 10 chips. These are your sample. How many chips of each color are there in the sample?

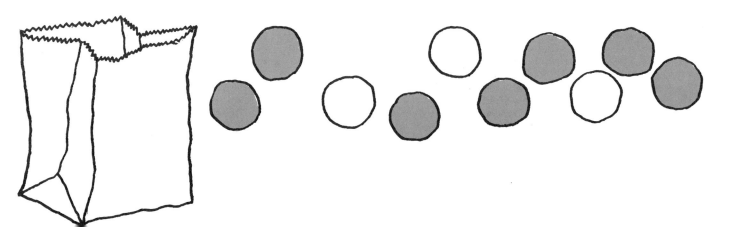

The sample will not help you to predict the number of each color of chip or marble in the bag. It will help you to predict the RATIO of the numbers of the two colors. Suppose you have red chips and white chips in the bag, and the sample shows 7 reds and 3 whites. This means you can predict, because of the sample, that about 7 out of 10, or about 70 per cent, of the chips in the bag are red.

That means, if I have 100 chips, 70 are red and 30 are white.

Probably.

The sample also tells you that if you were to draw 1 chip from the bag, the probability of its being red is about 7 in 10.

What predictions can you make because of your sample?

Now, replace that first sample. Shake the bag, and draw another 10 chips out. What predictions can you make, now, about the next chip you may draw from the bag? Is this prediction based on both of your samples? Try a few more samples of 10 chips each.

Then, dump out all the chips and count the two colors. How well did your samples compare to the ratio of the colors?

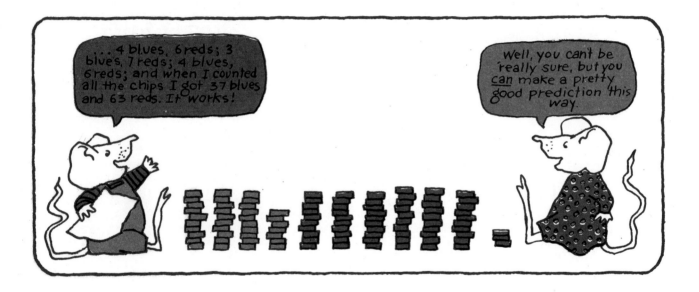

Did you find that with more samples—that is, more data—your predictions about the color of the "next" chip improved? Did your predictions about the ratio of the two colors get better?

You can say the same about the weatherman I mentioned at the beginning of this book. The more data he has, the more sure he can be about his predictions. "Sure" is really not the best word to use here. Scientists and mathematicians say, "The more data we have, the more CONFIDENT we are about our predictions."

But no matter how much data the scientist has about some natural event, he can never say he is completely confident about his prediction. That is, he can never say that some pattern of events will continue for sure.

All the air in a room might collect in one corner of the room. But, most probably it won't. There are many data that say this won't happen.

A ball thrown into the air might keep right on going out into space. But it most probably will come back down. Again, there are many data to back up the prediction.

If you come to the supper table with dirty hands and face, you might get away with it. But probably you will have to wash.

There are many data to back up this prediction.

ABOUT THE AUTHOR

Charles F. Linn teaches mathematics at Oswego State College in New York. He also works with students who will graduate and become teachers of mathematics. The author of numerous books in various fields of mathematics, Mr. Linn has also written *Estimation,* another book in Crowell's Young Math Series.

Charles Linn lives in Oswego, near the campus, with his wife, Nancy, and their five chlidren, Jeff, Jenny, Holly, Heather, and Susan.

ABOUT THE ILLUSTRATOR

Wendy Watson found it a challenge to put the subject matter of PROBABILITY into concrete, clear, and interesting illustrations for young children. "I was never much of a mathematician," she tells us, "so I tried to portray this book in a way that would have caught even my attention and interest as a child."

Miss Watson has written, edited, and adapted books for children and has illustrated nearly three dozen books, many of which have been chosen by the American Institute of Graphic Arts for its children's book shows. Born and raised on a farm in Vermont, Wendy Watson now lives with her husband in New York City.